A Small Business Owner's Guide to Digital Marketing

The proven set of strategies and tactics I used to drive leads, create more qualified buyers, and generate over $100MM in sales.

By Troy S. Scott

Copyright © 2017 Troy Scott | Scott Enterprises, LLC

All rights reserved. No part of this book may be used or reproduced by any means, graphic, electronic, or mechanical (including any information storage retrieval system) without the express written permission from the author, except in the case of brief quotations for use in articles and reviews wherein appropriate attribution of the source is made.

ISBN-13:
978-1976219092

ISBN-10:
1976219094

For bulk purchase and for booking, contact:

Attn: Troy Scott

Scott Enterprises, LLC
P.O. Box 28082
San Jose, CA 95159
669.223.0076

info@completeonlinestrategy.com

Because of the dynamic nature of the Internet, web addresses or links contained in this book may have been changed since publication and may no longer be valid.

Hi. Troy Scott here. I've always believed in transparency, so I am disclosing that I've included certain products and links to those products in the digital version of this book that I will earn an affiliate commission for any purchases you make as a direct result of my link. My goal with the book is to help educate you on the possibilities that exist for small business owners in practically any field, but please understand I am doing this as a for-profit business.

You should assume that any links leading you to products or services are affiliate links that I will receive compensation from just to be safe.

Having said that, there are millions of products and services on the web that are designed to help businesses of all sizes. I only promote those products or services that I have investigated and truly feel deliver value to you. Examples would include, BASE CRM, Kajabi, SEMRush Get Response and ClickFunnels.

Please note that I have not been given any free products, services, or anything else by these companies in exchange for mentioning them in this book. The only consideration is in the form of affiliate commissions when my clients use these products. Furthermore, if these products did not work for my clients, I would not have included them as great solutions to solving real digital marketing problems. Simply put, they're in this book because they work.

Cheers,

Troy S. Scott

Table of Contents

Introduction   1

   Welcome to the Small Business Owner's Guide to Digital Marketing

   Let's get started!   5

Overview of this Book   7

   How I Got Started   13

   Developing a Complete Online Strategy   20

   Getting from Point A to Point B   26

   Mapping out Your Business   27

The Framework   31

   Finding Baseline (Core vs. General KPIs)   33

   Creating Your Marketing Systems   35

   Operating Systems vs. Marketing Systems   36

   The System Tools   36

The 10-Point Checklist — 39

1. Content Creation — 40
2. Local SEO (Search Engine Optimization) — 42
3. AdWords Compliant Landing Pages — 44
4. Inbound Call Tracking & Recording — 51
5. Web Traffic & Conversion Metrics — 54
6. CRM Integration (Lead & Data Management) — 59
7. Marketing Automation (List Management) — 63
8. Lead Capture Pages — 64
9. Website Monitoring and Backups — 67
10. Set Up Monthly Reporting — 68

The 5-Step Outline — 71

Overview of the 5-Step Content Marketing Blueprint — 72

1. Foundation | Understanding Your Buyer's Journey — 72
2. Content | Targeting Your Avatar — 74
3. Evangelize | Publish, Syndicate & Communicate — 75
4. Automate | The Power of a System — 76
5. Scale & Optimize | Traffic & Congruency — 76

In the Trenches	79
The 5-Step Process in Action	79
Lead Nurturing vs. Buying Leads	88
10-Step Quick Start Guide	91
The Power of Outsourcing Your Marketing	93
The $2.1MM Case Study (Enter "The Buyer's Journey")	96
The $2,495 Per Month Employee	96
Real Case Studies of Success (Free Videos)	101
About the Author	103

FREE - Bonus Training

This book includes **video training** and a **Content Marketing Blueprint**

Visit these Google short links to learn more

Please note: All links are Case Sensitive

https://goo.gl/mXeDuu

Introduction

Welcome to the Small Business Owner's Guide to Digital Marketing

Hi, I'm Troy Scott. Thank you for taking the time to purchase this book. I'm truly grateful you did.

Over the last 10 years, I've designed, managed, and executed marketing programs that have generated over $100MM in B to C residential home improvement sales for Northern California.

My hope is that you can take what I present here and apply these strategies and tactics to your business.

If there is one thing that spending over $10MM on marketing has taught me, it's that you need to have a system in place to make things work. Otherwise, it can feel like you're just spinning your wheels.

I know this firsthand because that's how I used to feel before I understood how all this stuff works.

In 2010, I took the bold step away from more traditionally-used online marketing practices to develop a specific content marketing strategy around products we sold.

This overview details the systems and strategies I've successfully deployed to drive leads, educate prospects, and to ultimately create more qualified buyers.

When you deploy the power of content marketing, your prospects can engage with the information they want and need while your brand starts to build trust and authority.

When you combine this strategy with marketing automation, you can reap even bigger rewards.

Over time, by building on this one core strategy (content marketing), I've dramatically improved results across key performance metrics, such as:

- Geographic market share
- Creating better and more qualified buyers
- More efficient & effective lead generation
- Achieving total control of marketing data
- Delivering higher closing rates to sales

This book was written to help other small business owners like you establish the core elements of a winning digital marketing strategy and develop a similar framework for your business.

Before any of that took place, back in 2006, I decided to pivot away from the start-up culture of Silicon Valley and dive headfirst into the world of small business marketing—first as a VP of Marketing, then later as a digital marketing consultant.

When I first started in digital marketing, I quite literally overnight found myself in charge of a seven-figure advertising budget and had no way to track anything. The business was in the home improvement sector and completely foreign to me. It was only a handful of years old and beginning to see early success.

Instead of straight web conversions for leads, we leaned on TV and direct response marketing to get the phone to ring. From there, we set up in-home sales appointments.

To make things even more interesting, the company was operating without any sales or marketing infrastructure whatsoever. Zero, zip, nada.

Well, unless you count printed-out Excel sheets attached to a clipboard. Whoever answered the inbound calls wrote the name, phone number, and maybe an email address on it.

That's where I started.

I literally had to learn everything on fly, just like everyone else trying to run a business out there. It was trial by fire.

However, what I didn't realize at the time and have come to appreciate now is that every new business goes through this.

The early framework of reporting (Excel spreadsheets) is exactly how most small businesses start, especially when it comes to tracking sales and marketing data. In fact, even today when I start working with new clients, many are still stuck in this phase or stuck on what to do next.

It's still quite common to see, even today, many companies missing reporting infrastructure and rarely in command of their marketing data.

I get it. I was there.

This book will show you how to find and establish your baseline framework to build off of. It will give you a step-by-step process map and help you build a digital marketing plan. My hope is that you will discover new strategies and structured frameworks to improve the marketing of your business.

It's a little peek into what I learned, the systems I created, and the marketing elements I used to dominate a local geo-fenced business in the San Francisco Bay Area marketplace.

After we establish baseline and the tools you need to build it out, this book will discuss the five-step process I use (and still work with) to help other business owners generate leads and create more qualified buyers by leveraging these new technology and marketing automation tools put in place as your framework.

I'm going to completely break down the details of this digital marketing plan. I'll discuss in great detail the top, middle, and bottom of our funnel strategy and map out the five-step process.

I've also created a content marketing blueprint for you to download, model, and implement into your business. Finish by watching the case study videos, which will help you even further. Just visit https://goo.gl/mXeDuu.

Let's get started!

Here is what to expect in this book so you get the most out of it and your expectations are met.

First, it's interactive. There are lots of opportunities for you to go click out and learn more about the tools by digging deeper into the content and gaining access to even more information.

Second, this book is for business. It's intended to help you grow, produce highly qualified leads, and help you make more money.

Third, it's for implementers. You'll see there are *lots* of ideas that you can use to grow any business in any industry, country, or language. These systems take time to build and don't work overnight, but as you will see, they do work.

Fourth, this book wasn't intended to be a NY Times #1 Bestseller. It's designed to start a conversation with you, give you and I a chance to get to know each other better, and develop a trust and bond that will ultimately help us decide if we will work together someday.

Fifth, this is a book that's short, but packed with implementable content and lots of ideas. My intention and the purpose of this book is to show you a powerful way to market your business, generate more qualified leads, close more deals, and leverage cool marketing technologies.

Having said that, if you like what you read or most of what you read, I'd absolutely, positively love to hear from you, get to know you better, and have you post a success story, picture, or video and comment on my Facebook page: Facebook.com/TroyScottGroup.

The best way to start a relationship with me will be to visit the web links in this book, join me for the free training masterclasses, and learn more about how to grow your business and brand.

Sincerely,

Troy S. Scott, San Jose, California, USA

P.S. If you enjoy this book or find it useful, I'll be very grateful if you post a short review on Amazon. Your support makes a difference, and I read all the reviews personally so I can make this book even better. If you'd like to leave a review, just visit this link: https://goo.gl/neHjWG

Thanks again for your support!

Overview of this Book

The biggest shift I've seen most small business owners have to adapt to is moving off the spreadsheet and accepting that they need to create a marketing system.

Another major issue I see is committing what I call "random acts of marketing," which means the company will turn its marketing on and off sporadically. The company turns it on, gets leads, and then stops.

I understand that there are a lot of reasons for this. Oftentimes, it is due to the seasonality of the business, production capabilities, or company bandwidth.

Hear this: the single most powerful action a local business owner can take is committing to advertising all year long.

Why? Because when you leverage paid advertising and marketing automation systems and develop a monthly content publishing cycle, you can actually fortify and create an active growing list of prospects.

You can also answer many of the questions that the non-committed "tire-kickers" (the group of your buyers just doing research and not ready to buy) are looking for answers on and give them opportunities to actively engage in your content.

Once I understood the dynamics of this process, we found that we could still market in the slow months when sales actually fell off and still benefit from the folks in "research mode" who would search out our solutions and then opt-in to our content offers, which gave us a way to stay connected with them.

Over time, I began to see the true value of developing "marketing systems" rather than looking at my marketing as just paying for and buying leads. A prospect custom-branded to our company through our content was much more than a lead. When properly nurtured, a high percentage of these folks would eventually become buyers.

The big paradigm shift came when we started to look at these efforts from the perspective of a true marketing funnel and started developing our first few pieces of content strategically developed for one purpose: opt-ins. This is how we created our first set of free guides.

By free guides (white papers, lead magnets, or whatever your industry calls them), I'm talking about content that is relevant to your marketing target "avatar" or your core demographic group of potential buyers.

We started with just two guides titled: "The 8 Facts You Should Know" and "The 22 Questions You Should Ask." Both of them focused on common questions our prospects wanted answers to.

Why send a salesperson out to answer questions when we wanted them going out and closing deals? When you can answer questions for your prospects within your marketing channels and deliver that content as a strategy, the barrier to closing the sale shrinks, and you begin to create more qualified buyers.

We performed research around the keywords and phrases our prospects were searching for and began to optimize blog posts and create content around those topics. We knew what people were looking for when they were doing searches for the products and services we offered, so we just created free guides around those terms.

We started with just two at first, then expanded to where we are today, with a total of 27 different types of "opt-in" downloadable content. The content we created would ultimately lead prospects to opt-in to landing pages. These pages were connected to specific marketing funnels and designed to segment prospects into five distinctly different buyer groups.

From there, our marketing automation and lead-nurturing systems provided a steady drip of content. In this business, we had five distinctly different marketing messages written for a specific avatar or persona around that specific product.

Not only did our prospects benefit from the content we were creating, the business and local brand benefited as well.

Over time, our brand was perceived as the expert or the authority in the market simply because we were becoming the local go-to destination for answering prospects' questions in the form of free guides and blog content.

All by simply giving away our best content for free.

This info-marketing process began to address common questions that would normally bog down our call center. Since our guides addressed these common questions, over time, we had positioned our brand on **value rather than price,** which, in turn, allowed us to demand premium prices.

Once we focused on marketing this way, the other massive upside was discovering that our marketing automation and follow-up systems began to literally create more qualified buyers.

I'll share real data with you along with actual case studies that will showcase a number of success metrics we began to see. For example, this process has led to our call center converting inbound prospect calls to in-home appointments at an 86% conversion rate.

This process moved prospects along a "buyer's journey" to becoming prequalified and ready for our sales reps.

As our prospects downloaded our free guides, they received our automated email messaging. I know—boring old email.

This process during peak seasonality produced ready-for-appointment web lead forms converting at the 41% range and booking appointments at as high as an 86% conversion rate.

These conversions are not free guide opt-in numbers; these are folks who were coming back to the site and filling out a "ready for appointment" form.

As this process unfolded, the other obvious upside was seeing a progressively increasing closing percentage with our sales reps.

The data on aggregate saw a nearly 100% increase with average closing rates over time moving from the 20s to the 40s.

What was actually happening was that we began to move prospects from the investigation (top of the funnel) mode to the interested (middle of the funnel) mode, which, as you will see, changed the dynamics of the business dramatically.

After adopting and deploying this content marketing strategy and seeing great success early on, we added a more focused approach that I will outline later in the book, the concept of creating and implementing what we call the "buyer's journey."

It's the process of creating and developing content around information marketing strategies that are aimed at each stage of the buying process.

Around 2010, I adopted the free guide approach to lead generation and committed to going all in on content marketing. Our content was then syndicated in the form of blogs, marketing videos, and free guides that users would opt in for.

I focused on creating a marketing funnel with three core parts: a top, a middle, and a bottom, and we started seeing some incredible results.

With this new approach, the data that was really driving the business had become much easier to navigate and more importantly, easier to take action on.

By far the biggest outcome of adopting this process was the ability to take command of the marketing data with true visibility instead of letting the business control me by just buying leads and hoping for the best.

By "control," I mean that this process and system took the guesswork out of determining ROI by advertising channel. It gave me a new outlook instead of looking for ways to just "buy leads" as a result of marketing. It was now a data-driven system.

The activities that drive leads, phone calls, appointments, and sales all begin at the top of the funnel. How your company first engages with a prospect, the opt-in phase, and the follow-up process are all part of the middle of the funnel. The bottom is all about the conversion step to the sale.

The buyer's journey and how the process is structured can have huge impacts on your business.

By the time you finish this book, you will have a blueprint that you can take action on. I completely break down what I have learned, the systems I created, and what was required to elevate a local brand to over $100MM in sales.

We'll start by developing a firm foundation in what I call a "baseline reading" using simple tools like Google Analytics. It's still shocking how many businesses overlook this amazing free tool.

In many ways, analytics are what makes the world go 'round — particularly in the data-driven environment that we're now living in. According to Forbes, more data was created during the last two years than in all of the time in human history leading up to it combined!

That's a terrific position to be in if you're a business trying to learn more about your customers, but it's also an overwhelming time for people who were never prepared to make "number crunching" a full-time job. As a result of this massive influx of data, analytics services (and particularly Google Analytics) have become an invaluable tool for people, content marketers in particular, over the last decade.

From there, I will then showcase the structure of our marketing automation and list-building tools to show you how we use segmented sales funnels to separate our marketing messages to solution-specific buyers.

Content marketing strategies provide a true marketing win/win in the marketplace. Combine this approach with today's incredible technology, and these types of online systems become conversion machines where efficiencies improve exponentially.

How I Got Started

Over the past 20 years, I've worked on and with a variety of different types of business models. My first startup was with my brother-in-law selling into big-box stores using an overseas supply chain that sold through to consumers as a hardware peripheral component.

From that business, I moved on to web development and SAAS (software as a service) products, where we developed (too late as it turned out) an Angie's List type of service for the home improvement space.

From there, I became a founding team member of a now-defunct personal finance management tool company that my step brother (entrepreneurial family) developed as a mobile and desktop app, which was released on iTunes and Google Play.

I wouldn't discover my true passion for digital marketing until years later after another startup project ended.

The relationship I developed with one of my first investors extended into a job offer at the relatively new home improvement company I mentioned at the beginning of this book, which is based in San Jose, California.

The opportunity involved developing processes and building marketing systems in a practicable application environment (fancy talk for spending money on advertising and then seeing what would happen), which, in turn, gave me a marketing platform to test, fail, and pivot whenever it was required.

This process of tweaking and changing marketing strategies year after year paved the way for me to discover what worked, what failed, and what to avoid.

My experience has evolved into helping other businesses create and execute digital marketing plans. It's been rewarding helping other entrepreneurs achieve great results with the small things that can have big impacts.

In many ways, the technology of today has made digital marketing plans much easier to use and set up; however, at the same time, they can still be quite overwhelming and complicated for business owners to navigate if they don't speak the language.

And that is exactly why I wrote this book.

I've always been a marketing nerd, and I feel lucky (more like blessed and grateful) to be in the types of environments that stimulated my intellectual growth and allowed for the practical application of new skills.

Whether it was reading marketing books, following technology newsletters, attending trade shows and live events, or investing in online training courses and certification programs—all of these activities helped educate me on how these new platforms worked.

However, nothing beats running your own digital ad campaigns and seeing real people click on your advertisements. The excitement that comes from tracking the progress of the clicks and then ultimately converting those clicks into sales can be addictive. Yup #supergeeky.

It's pretty exciting when you're in the trenches and have the opportunity to build campaigns and see the results of how all these systems work together as one big marketing funnel, driving traffic and converting complete strangers into buyers.

Ok, let's talk real about how it all started, the crazy early days and the reality that came about by truly being in the right place at the right time... you know the old saying:

"Luck is what happens when **preparation meets opportunity.**"

This quote has often been attributed to Seneca, a Roman philosopher. It can teach us that luck is something we create and completely depends on our perspective.

In early 2006 and continuing over the past 10 years, I've had the opportunity to "build out" localized marketing campaigns with fairly large advertising budgets by local marketing standards.

These annual budgets ranged on average anywhere from $750k to peaking at a high of over $1,000,000 per year.

In the first few years, the big marketing push was mostly all direct response TV advertising.

Of course, we invested in all the other staples at the time: direct marketing, magazines, newspapers, and event marketing. Yup, we had a website; however, it was very basic and completely static. Back in the day, some called those sites "brochureware" — flat and static, just information.

The direct response TV opportunity gave me the chance to experience local network television with in-studio live broadcasts and to work with an ad agency producing the local TV ads. From there, it was all about learning the art of long-form direct response advertising by scripting, producing, and even being the spokesperson in numerous 30-minute infomercials.

At the time, TV broadcasting of local infomercials were a big deal for our market, and it gave us access to a large audience and produced great results.

The infomercial days were nuts though, just insane... we drove "Act Now" offers as the CTA (call to action) at a time when we were the first to market with these products that no one had ever seen on TV before around 2005–2007.

It was pure insanity—the wild west really.

It was quite literally 30 minutes of phone calls just raining down on us. We had no hope of catching them all. I remember we would tell the entire office staff to brace for the onslaught when the show went live at 10 a.m. on a Saturday…

No call center, no phone system really, just an old-school hunt-group type of setup that directed all inbound calls to any available phone that was not in use.

If all the phone lines were busy, we missed the calls, and those phones rang off the hook. I don't think we even had a voicemail system for messages, so we missed a lot of calls.

But we got a lot of leads… like thousands of them.

Those infomercial days where the first in a series of wake-up calls for me after becoming the vice president of marketing.

That's when I discovered the archaic reporting systems in place, or should I say, the lack of reporting systems in place.

For example, at the end of the 30-minute broadcast, the dust would settle, and our total lead reporting system consisted of nothing more than scribbled names on three or four different clipboards with multiple pages.

Each page contained a list of contacts that had grown as fast as the people answering the phones could write information down before moving on to another call.

And the questions... so many questions. Every caller asked at least two of the same questions every time: "How much is it?" "How do you install it?" etc., all of which were great questions to ask except our folks had to end the call as soon as possible in order to grab the next line that was ringing... good times.

Something to consider is that even that insanely broken system still worked.

That's how it started: no tracking, nothing digital, and just about everything on paper.

I was grateful, however, that I had spent a number of months cutting my teeth as a sales rep for the company first.

This proved to be a great move, as it provided real insight into what happens to our prospects after they set an appointment with us and what takes place when the rep shows up. It was valuable to understand what expectations (or lack thereof) the prospects had at the time the appointment was booked.

After a few months of running appointments and selling deals, I began to notice gaps in our front-end marketing process. Many of the same common questions were coming up over and over that could be addressed much earlier in the marketing process.

It was a valuable experience to learn what it was like for our prospects to go from being interested in our products to the appointment-setting phase to the close.

I will save the details for later chapters, but suffice it to say that after years and years of iterations, today this business runs entirely on systems and is the envy of the industry it leads.

Today, we can stay on top of this business by checking a few apps and simply tapping through dashboards on any smartphone. Yes, it is super geeky awesome.

I can see which advertising channel is producing the most leads or how many appointments the call center set that day or the number of projects being installed.

I can tell you how many conversions our website had down to the number of appointments our PPC (Google AdWords) buy has produced for the day, month, quarter, or year.

In other words, I have complete visibility of this company from the top to bottom, all because we view this business as a top, middle, and bottom of the funnel operation.

In fact, these marketing and production systems have grown into predictable revenue models that consistently, year after year, produce seven and eight figures in annual sales.

I'm excited to share this information with you, as I believe if you can take what I lay out here and implement it into your business, you could have great results too.

Developing a Complete Online Strategy

Oftentimes, one of the biggest challenges for any business owner is grappling with the paradox of getting stuck working in the business versus working on the business.

In a later section, I'll talk about operating systems vs. marketing systems to address this point.

However, generally speaking, if you can set up a marketing system that requires minimal in-house management to run, you'll be freed up to work on your business instead of in your business.

In the early days, I was doing *everything*. Content creation, blogging, video production, managing the PPC buys, and at its peak, running over 78 live promo events… I mean everything.

Believe me, it took a few years for me to actually let go of all this stuff. I'm not a control freak; I just wanted it done right, and I stressed myself out way more than I needed to.

In retrospect, it worked out, but I did hang on to managing projects way too long when I absolutely needed to let go of them and get out of the way.

For me personally, one of the single biggest adjustments I made was outsourcing the management of time-consuming tasks like content creation, paid traffic management, and other "working in my business" roles that kept me from doing "working on my business," big-picture, thinking type of activities.

More directly, this book is about creating and setting up digital marketing systems that you simply manage for the results you're after—systems that deliver data, so you, the business owner, understand what is actually happening with your marketing efforts and can make better advertising decisions.

Understanding your web traffic, your lead flow, how your phone calls are being answered, your sales conversions, your follow-up methods, and even managing customers reviews are important tasks that you should have a grasp on.

The automation is the cool part because once it's set up, you just tweak it from time to time. The implementation, on the other hand, can be daunting, especially for business owners who are afraid of change. Many think that their business is running just fine, or worse, don't think they will get left behind by their competitors who are taking action to implement today's awesome marketing tools.

Setting these systems up can be quite valuable; in fact, they can actually increase the value of your company. Creating these types of systems can be powerful incentives if you want an exit strategy by acquisition. If your business is profitable and has proven systems that are managing the infrastructure, the business can be much easier to sell.

If you're just getting started, these systems don't need to be super complicated either.

Take websites, for example. Today, simple Wordpress themes have eliminated the need to pay for expensive programmers. These themes can be cookie-cutter or completely customizable, and will typically work for any type of business.

Need an e-commerce platform? Shopify is your go-to system. Obviously, not every business can use Wordpress themes, especially if your model requires a comprehensive UI (user interface) to sell or transact on. But you get the idea here.

I'm talking in general terms for most businesses. The Wordpress platform uses a "plug-in tool" (software you add to the site) to help solve other website-related issues, such as backing up your website data, collecting leads, or syndicating of your content. If you want your Wordpress theme to do something specific, there is a good chance a plug-in will be there for it.

Obviously, Wordpress is not the only solution out there, but today, it's more than enough to work in most business environments, complete with the flexibility to work on any device, since your site better be mobile-friendly. If you're still using an old-school website format that "works just fine" because you're one of those "I don't like change" people, you really need to be paying attention to Google Analytics.

It's a small example of little things that can have big impacts. Chances are you're losing website traffic due to visitors looking at your site on a mobile device and bouncing... as in leaving your site and never coming back. I'll touch on this important marketing component later in the book. Take a look at this chart (Fig. 1) below.

Notice how much web traffic is coming from mobile use—41%? What would happen if this site was not optimized for mobile? This would have a negative impact on conversions.

Snapshot of Monthly Website Traffic by Device

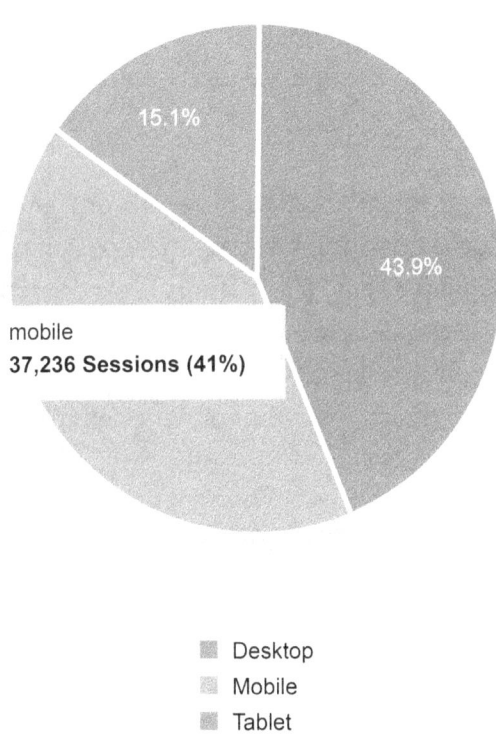

- Desktop
- Mobile
- Tablet

FIG. 1 GOOGLE ANALYTICS

Making sure your site is optimized for mobile users should be at the top of the list when building out your digital marketing plan.

Another great technology trend has been the ubiquitous adoption of API technology, which connects digital solutions to virtually any other digital solution. This technology has made creating systems easier than ever before. Simply put, API technology allows users to connect applications together and automate workflows via custom scripts.

The upside is that real marketing problems can be solved with thousands of solutions in this brave new world of cloud-based programming. Take Zapier, for example. This company has a gigantic library of preconfigured "Zaps" (API scripts) that easily plug into hundreds of other apps and can be configured and activated into systems you may already be running. And many of these Zaps are free (Fig. 2)!

This is a great example of what APIs can do for businesses that want to connect marketing solutions together.

Over the years, when speaking directly to business owners, I've consistently heard the same issue come up over and over: that all of this is confusing and overwhelming.

The common roadblock for many business owners is that new technology ultimately means change. For many, this signals a reluctance to let go of control because it's new and unfamiliar to them. The old "but we've always done it this way and it's working just fine" excuse is a very common response to adding new marketing technologies to a business.

A SMALL BUSINESS OWNER'S GUIDE TO DIGITAL MARKETING

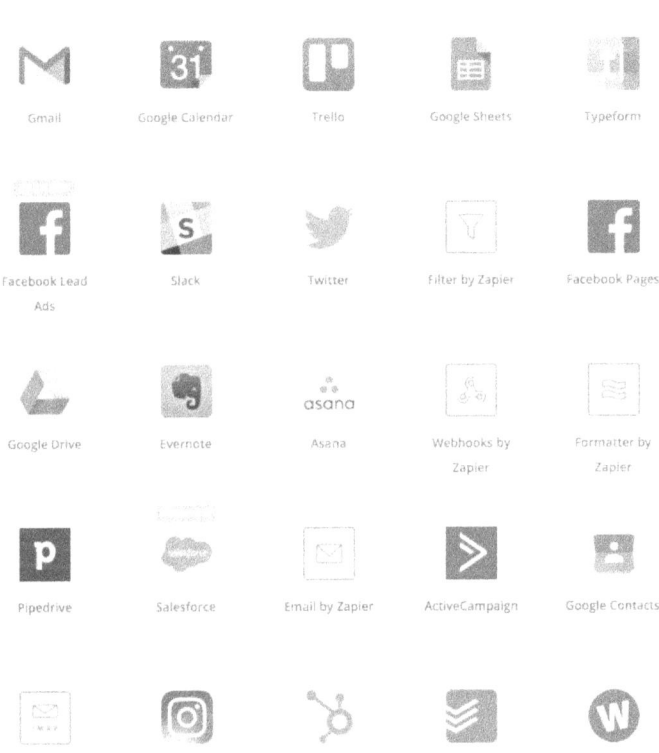

FIG. 2 ZAPIER

The new reality for just about every small business today is that they must adopt digital marketing plans in order to compete, get control of their marketing data, and perhaps most important of all, use that data to make better marketing decisions.

Getting from Point A to Point B

The first thing you have to do is take a look at the systems you already have in place. Is your system as simple as the lead flow clipboard I referenced earlier in the book?

It really doesn't matter, because even if you think you don't have system in place... you have a system.

What I want you to do is to visualize your current lead flow process. When a lead comes into your business (we will start with the easy one) in the form of a phone call, what happens?

When your phone rings, who answers it? What happens with the call information? Does it go right into an Excel file? Does it get typed into your CRM (Customer Relationship Management) software and sent to sales for the follow-up call?

I love exploring this process when I first meet with and ask the owners about it. Every time this process is introduced, owners see their businesses like never before. If you want some clarity on what you think is happening, take the time to map out your business.

Mapping out Your Business

Most business owners have never done this. It's amazing what happens when you take the time to map it out.

I use a simple cloud tool at https://www.draw.io to map my clients. Using APIs, I can connect these drawings to Google Drive and Box.net among others for maximum sharing input.

Take a look at the image below for this example. The number of boxes here isn't the focus. You need to actually visualize your current lead process, call process, sales process, etc.

Draw out a diagram of how that inbound lead turns into a sale for your business, and share it with your management and ask for feedback. You may find little inefficiencies that can be corrected to increase productivity. You may not realize it, but you do have a system in place. When you take the time to draw it out, you will see things differently.

This is a very basic Leadflow Diagram (Fig.3)

At the end of the day, whatever your map looks like is the current system you have in place. This is point A, where you are at now.

When you begin to look at your business from a digital perspective as one big marketing funnel, your entire perspective on your business can and will change.

Map Out Your Lead Flow

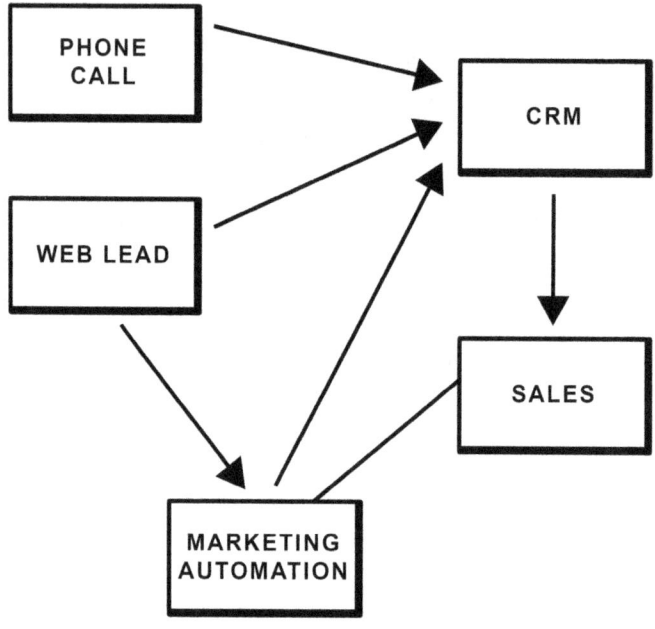

FIG. 3 LEADFLOW DIAGRAM

Once you add in marketing automation, paid traffic, and clear conversion paths that are tied to key performance indicators (KPIs) as they relate to your digital marketing plan, you will have moved from Point A to Point B.

Point B is the new perspective you will have on your business.

The Framework

We need to get to a place where your marketing data is clear and actionable. I call this beginning phase your baseline.

I'm going to lay out all of the data points I look at as they relate to our entire marketing funnel in the business we're outlining in this book. We have all of the KPIs that I track for the digital marketing plan for this business in place.

I ultimately focus on the core KPI (top level) numbers that will bubble up as a result of the cumulative general data points below:

- All advertising channels (all phone calls tracked with dedicated numbers)
    - TV, print, direct marketing, live events, brochures, etc.
- Paid traffic (paid search advertisements)
    - Adwords, Facebook, Youtube, remarketing, etc.
- Website traffic
    - Organic search
        - Google, Bing, Yahoo

- Referrals
    - Links on other sites
- Social media
    - Facebook, Twitter, LinkedIn, etc.
- Email marketing
    - Drip campaigns, monthly newsletters
- Direct traffic
    - Manually-entered URLs
- Other campaigns
    - Retargeting

- Total lead flow
    - *How many **leads** came in for the month*
- Total phone calls
    - *How many **calls** came in for the month*
- Total appointments set
    - *How many **appointments set** for the month*
- Total appointments ran
    - *How many **appointments ran** for the month*
- Closing percentage
    - *How many sales*
- Total Sales
    - *How much we sold that month*

The folks that didn't buy from us are still in our marketing automation systems and will continue to get our monthly published content until they buy (which we see happen a lot, sometimes a year or more later) or opt out of our marketing messages altogether.

Finding Baseline (Core vs. General KPIs)

There is a certain feeling of calm that will come over you when you are in command of your marketing data.

Once you're in a place where a baseline has been established, your marketing budget is easier to plan for as it relates to forecasting on next year's sales.

I tend to use all of those data points that I outlined above to measure out baseline metrics for YoY (Year Over Year), MoM (Month Over Month), or quarterly success metrics.

Typically, I will focus on two types of KPI groups:

1. General KPIs

    a. What I outlined above; the raw marketing data from all marketing channels to measure performance

2. Core KPIs

    a. For the business model outlined in this book, the raw marketing data turns into four core KPIs.

        i. Total appointments set

        ii. Total appointments ran

    iii. Closing %

    iv. Total sales

Notice that leads are not part of my core KPI list?

I really don't care about leads in this business. Sure, leads are vital; however, leads are just a byproduct of marketing. Leads for this company typically stay locked inside marketing automation until they move to the next step in the system and become an appointment, an income-generating activity for this type of business. They're not counted as a core KPI. I can't make money with a lead.

However, leads are the lifeblood of the middle of the funnel where our marketing automation and monthly newsletters are used to stay in contact with these prospects. They will raise their hands, so to speak, when they're ready for the next step of the buyer's journey, the appointment and sales consultation step, also known as the bottom of the funnel stage.

In order for this business to make money, we need to have appointments being set, actual presentations being made, deals getting closed, and projects being installed.

Both of these general and core KPI metrics are well-established and predictable for this business because we know our baseline numbers.

When I refer to baseline, I'm looking to establish a reference point that we can measure performance off of.

If I don't know my marketing performance numbers from September of last year, how am I going to measure my success or failure for September this year?

Did I overspend or underspend, or am I just buying leads and hoping for the best? Hope is not a success metric, the same for Facebook likes.

The first thing you need to do is get your baseline numbers established and recorded. Start tracking your core KPIs as soon as you can in order to better understand your seasonality and last year's success metrics.

Generally speaking, you can measure in three-year increments to establish trend lines and forecasting models. Obviously, that statement can vary greatly; however, generally speaking, a three-year block of data can tell you a lot about the business. Setting up these systems will help.

Creating Your Marketing Systems

Think about this for a second. In your business, do you have an operations department? Most companies do. It's typically where the hands-on or fulfillment part of sales takes place.

Depending on whether your business provides professional services or sells physical products, you're running another system to fulfill either the services or products that you've sold.

It's interesting to talk with business owners who know they need an operations system and then refuse to put the same emphasis on creating a marketing system.

Operating Systems vs. Marketing Systems

Your business is actually just one big operating system broken down into departments all working together as one finely tuned machine.

At least that's what we tell ourselves as business owners.

The obvious and more fun part of the business (I'll admit I'm biased) is the marketing system you need to have.

So let's take a look at the components needed to run a content marketing program.

The System Tools

Oftentimes when this process begins, when you begin mapping out your business and assessing the current systems, it's easy to lose track of just focusing on what you need to get started.

If you want one succinct short list minus the details, it would look like this:

- Content marketing
- Social media marketing
- Video marketing
- Media buying/traffic acquisition
- Testing & optimizing
- Email/marketing automation

These are the mainstays of today's digital marketing world. However, getting your business up and running without a clear roadmap can turn into a colossal waste of time if you're trying to do this on your own.

The 10-Point Checklist

To help guide you in developing your new digital marketing plan, I've created a ten-point checklist that includes the components I would build out if I had to start over building a new system from the ground up.

This approach is focused on a local small business serving a specific market niche or region.

I will detail this list in the in the coming pages.

1. Content Creation (blogging/free guides/newsletters)
2. Search engine optimization (60-point build-out)
3. PPC Adwords management (landing pages)
4. Dynamic call tracking & recording
5. Web traffic & conversion metrics
6. CRM integration (lead management)
7. Marketing automation with email follow-up to segment
8. Lead capture pages for free guides

9. Website monitoring and backup systems

10. Monthly reporting

Every business is different; however, fundamentally speaking, these are the 10 components every business that markets online will need to put in place.

1. Content Creation (You Need a Content Marketing Strategy)

You will need to identify the content that you will need for your funnel and then create a variety of different asset types. These could be PDF documents, blog posts, videos, or just about any type of content that will help to outline your value proposition.

In your business, what would work better? The free guide strategy or free explainer bridge videos?

In order to figure this out, you will need to determine your core top-of-the-funnel message and build your content around that.

Bridge videos are great because they can be quite personal and inviting as yet another layer of information to move your prospect to a conversion point. Here is an example of a bridge video that I recently created as an opt-in for one or our landing pages: https://goo.gl/VnLfwW

Here is another example—Free Guides (https://goo.gl/hyQene). The first two guides we built (those that I shared earlier in the book) were all about artificial grass. Remember, we started by creating just two: "The 8 Facts You Should Know Before Investing

In Artificial Grass" and "The 22 Questions You Should Ask Yourself Before Installing Artificial Grass." Both of these guides focused on common questions our prospects wanted answers to about artificial grass.

Pick one or both of these content delivery strategies and start creating the type of content that your prospects could benefit from learning about as it relates to your product or service.

What type of content do you need for your top-of-the-funnel giveaway offer? A free guide or a bridge video?

Once you have these offers created, what you need to do next is get them out to market. One of the most efficient ways to do this is by blog syndication.

This can be done in a number of really efficient ways.

First, remember when I spoke about Wordpress as a website platform and introduced the concept of plug-ins? Well, one very effective way to syndicate content is to create blog content inside of a Wordpress site and use syndication plug-ins.

One very effective tool I've used is OnlyWire. This software gives you instant reporting and analytics on your automatically syndicated posts that can be distributed to as many as 50 social platforms. With the scheduling post features in Wordpress, this allows you to create and plan out your content in scheduled increments.

Another great app is Buffer, which can manage social media posts in syndication form as well.

By using blog posts as your publishing platform, you can link to or embed related videos and other content and schedule the post to publish daily, weekly, or monthly.

As interested parties find your blog content, your blogs will have embedded CTA links that would allow users to opt in and, in turn, help you grow your email lists.

2. Local SEO (Search Engine Optimization)

There was a lot of talk recently when Google announced yet another update to its algorithm that affected content creators and their rankings. Here is the complete update: https://goo.gl/MvjQmg

It seems some folks are complaining that SEO is dead and gone, pointing to some of the facts related to recent updates.

I've not seen that to be the case. SEO works, you just need to do it correctly and consistently. Sure, it's gotten harder to rank, but a consistent approach to publishing SEO-driven optimized content works.

Basic SEO is the cornerstone of organic rankings, and aside from new signals and sophisticated algorithms (how Google sees and rates your site's content), nothing has really changed about it. Of course, there are many factors that go into ranking your site; however, as I said before, the basic premise has stayed consistent.

Consistently creating good quality content is what SEO is all about. In fact, good quality content properly aligned with the correct approach to publishing it always wins, and it's become even more important from a local ranking perspective.

I have a case study later in this book that will showcase a client of mine currently seeing a significant jump in organic search traffic as it relates to a properly executed SEO plan.

In fact, if you are so inclined, a great resource and great read for this type of information can be seen here on how properly executed SEO plans can work. This great case study is from one of my favorite SEO sites, Search Engine Land: https://goo.gl/876ZM8

The general outline of Search Engine Land's strategy is:

1. Start slow and take advantage of "easy wins."

2. Focus on securing a handful of strategic links to important pages.

3. Establish passive link acquisition channels to build momentum.

4. **You should be intentional about content creation and its impact on search.**

5. Level up over time and target higher-value opportunities.

I purposely highlighted **#4** on this list because it's all about quality content. It's always about quality content. Ideally, you should be publishing a minimum of two times to four times more a month if you're able to do so.

For the business we're outlining in this book, we publish as many as 12–15 blogs a month! Three times every week.

On-page SEO is the often-overlooked tool for small business owners. Since SEO takes much longer to show results, most business owners don't have the patience to wait the four to six months it takes to see results.

From what I've learned, business owners typically don't have the patience because they're stuck in the "random acts of marketing" phase I discussed earlier in the book.

They have not planned out or correctly budgeted building out their marketing systems.

It is easier to just buy your leads. However, depending on your niche, that can get expensive.

In today's local market, you need a fairly robust SEO build-out.

In fact, I would suggest that it has as many as 60 points of reference with all the nuances required. When searching out these types of services, make sure that you get documentation on exactly what the agency is going to build out for you.

3. AdWords Compliant Landing Pages

One of the best ways to drive new business is to advertise, and depending on your market niche, Google Adwords Pay-Per-Click can be a powerful ally to market your business.

However, keep in mind that if you plan to run paid search ads, you'll need to make sure your website's landing pages (the pages your ad will link to) are Google AdWords-compliant. This is required in order to get your ads published in AdWords. If you're looking for a deeper dive into this topic, this link goes into greater detail with examples and how-to steps. I'll detail some high-level points as they relate to this topic.

https://goo.gl/876ZM8

This part has to do with your landing page copy. You will need "footer-type" links that show Google you are a real site with connected links to your about us, privacy policy, and contact us pages.

Other commonly overlooked issues that come with paid traffic strategies are often related to setting up your campaign.

For a truly successful campaign, you must pay attention to the concept of **Congruency** and your keyword **Quality Score**.

Let's start with congruency. This concept is all about the flow of the ad copy as it relates to the content and related copy on the landing page.

Looking below, all three of these Google ads marked with arrows do a great job of including keywords in the copy for the related search phrase (Fig. 4).

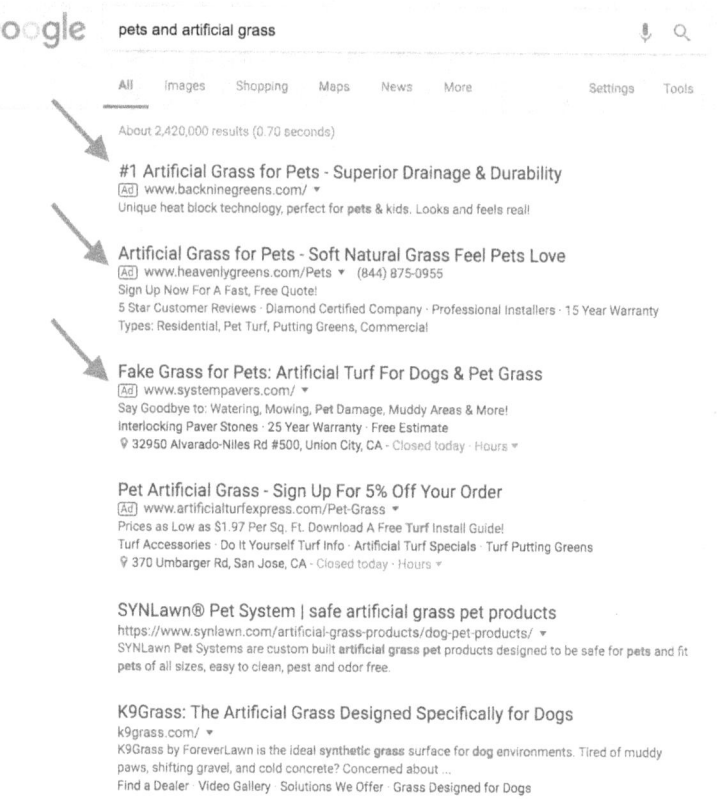

FIG. 4 SEARCH RESULTS

However, the top ad does not have congruency with the content copy on the landing page below (Fig. 5).

Looking at this landing page, there is zero reference to the core word being searched on (pets), which is most likely what the user's intent was—to actually learn more about artificial grass and pets. There is no mention or use of the words "dog" or "pets" anywhere on this landing page.

No mention or use of the words
"dog" or "pet" on this page

FIG. 5 LANDING PAGE COPY

In this example, we can see the power and importance of congruency, or making sure that your content is in alignment and matches the intent of the user. Your ads should speak to the on-page marketing copy and be congruently aligned.

When a user clicks through on ads (like the example above) and does not see the type of information he or she wants, the user simply clicks away, resulting in wasted ad spend and contributing to poor results.

Worse, the opportunity you had to convert the user is completely wasted delivering a negative ROI metric to what could have been a conversion. The ad campaign gets dinged as a fail when, in fact, the "keyword buy" (the term you chose to match the search) delivered the click-through to a page without the proper copy or imagery in place.

By referencing the above paid search result, "pets and artificial grass" (Fig. 4 above), you can see that this landing page meets and passes the congruency test.

This page below (Fig. 6) provides relevant content the user wants to see and read about based on the intent of the user's search terms.

The next big one is **Quality Score**.

This has to do with how relevant your PPC ad is. This is literally a score of not only congruency, but how relative your content is to the search term. Typically the higher your QS, the less expensive and more served your ad can become.

The Quality Score is an estimate of how relevant your ads, keywords, and landing page are to a person who sees your ad. Higher Quality Scores typically lead to lower costs and better ad positions. Follow this link to learn more about Quality Scores. https://goo.gl/FjyXkw

A SMALL BUSINESS OWNER'S GUIDE TO DIGITAL MARKETING   49

Artificial Turf for Dogs

What dog doesn't love a soft, grassy play area? Artificial grass looks and feels like the real thing, only it's better. Fake grass is perfect for pets and their friends, because it's designed specifically for dogs. And it's perfectly safe for your family and the environment, because it's non-toxic and allergen-free. With artificial grass, you can have a gorgeous yard and a happy canine.

Want to learn more? Download our Pet Case Study and see why your dog will love artificial grass like the dog below!

What dog doesn't love a soft, grassy play area? Fake grass for dogs looks and feels like the real thing, only it's better. Artificial turf is perfect for pets and their friends, because it's designed specifically for dogs. And it's perfectly safe for your family and the environment, because it's non-toxic and allergen-free. With artificial grass, you can have a gorgeous yard and a happy canine.

Busy dogs can turn natural lawn into a mess. Fake grass for dogs eliminates ugly yellow patches, bare spots, and holes. Give yourself a break, with beautiful artificial turf that's virtually maintenance free. And give your dog the year-round, weather-proof play area he deserves. Learn more now by downloading our pet case study.

FIG. 6 CORRECT PAGE CONTENT

This image is from within Google AdWords. Most accounts will need to add the Quality Score column in order for this data to show up on the dashboard or in reports (Fig. 7).

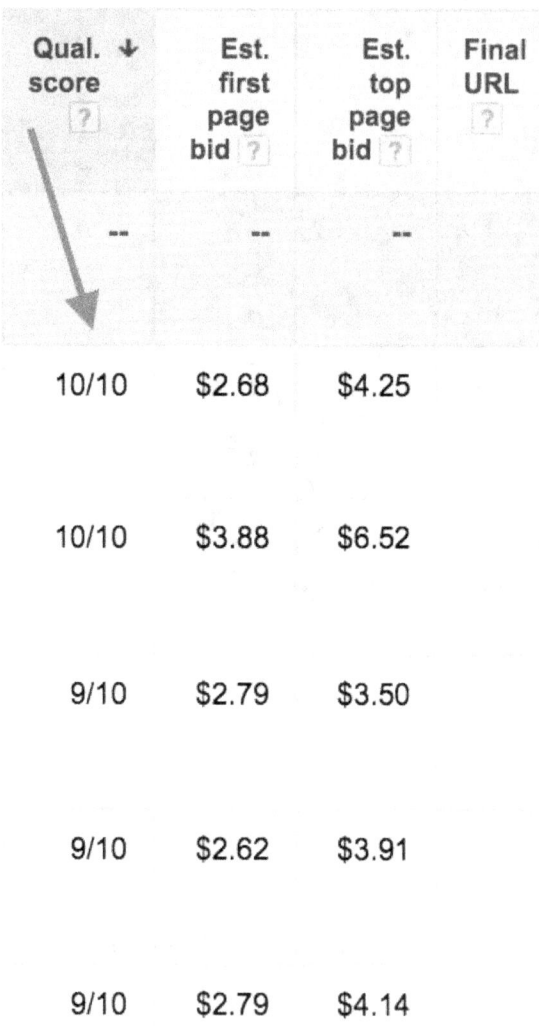

FIG. 7 QUALITY SCORE

4. Inbound Call Tracking & Recording

In my opinion, this is one of the most important and commonly overlooked digital tools most small businesses lack.

By far, one of the best investments you can make into your marketing system is to track and record all of your calls.

In years past, these types of sophisticated tracking systems were out of reach for many small businesses. However, the available technology of today provides businesses with a large variety to choose from.

With so many different types of solutions available, you can waste a lot of time learning all the different features and benefits that are available.

Here is a great list of solutions to get started with https://goo.gl/E2yNrg. Right at the top is one of my favorites, CallRail. I use CallRail with all of my clients since the functionality and integration features are fantastic.

This type of tracking delivers an entirely new dimension of marketing data. By providing both dynamic tracking numbers that track based on the advertising channel driving your web traffic (organic, paid, etc.), you can also measure ROI by advertising channel.

Another nice feature is adding static numbers that can be used in a number of different ways such as print ads, billboards, brochures, etc.

As you build out your systems, at some point, you will want to integrate this data in your CRM (customer relationship management) tools to manage your leads. Since CallRail works directly with Zapier (the API solution we discussed in an earlier section), the options are nearly limitless, making integrations a snap with CallRail's feature-rich functionality.

The other bonus is having the calls recorded.

Beyond the obvious benefit of recorded calls, the serendipity of this feature is actually listening to how your employees are answering inbound sales calls.

Do you know how your prospects are being treated when they call? I've had clients tell me the folks answering the phones are awesome, no problems there! Sadly, they need to hear it for themselves before they make changes.

Oftentimes, we find folks veering off the marketing message or worse, treating callers poorly.

This is a powerful tool; not only does it put your employees on notice that their calls are being recorded, but it gives you a tool to monitor how your calls are being handled.

The other great benefit is that the recordings become a fantastic training tool! Recorded calls can provide a "real-time" environment for handling unruly customers and he-said-she-said issues, and saving your rockstar employee calls to listen to over and over can be fun.

This solution is cloud-based and has a great mobile app. Here's what the dashboard looks like (Fig. 8):

CallRail Dashboard

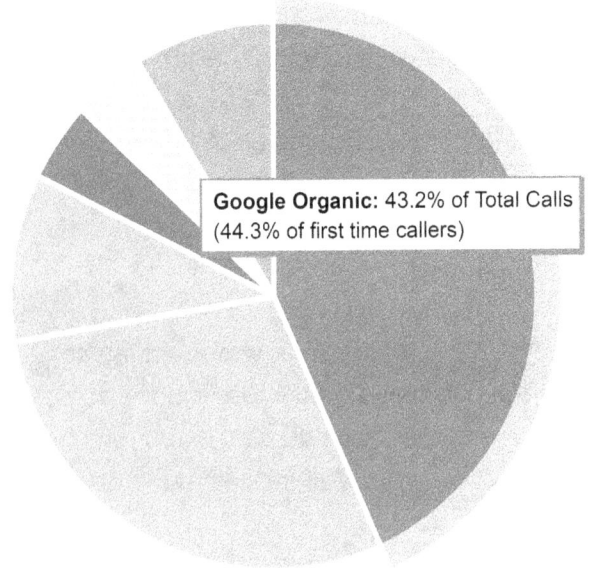

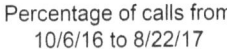

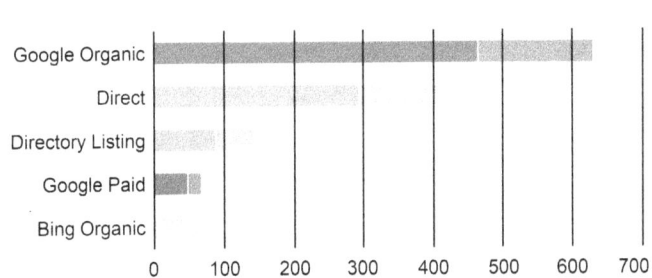

FIG. 8 CALLRAIL DASHBOARD

5. Web Traffic & Conversion Metrics

Do you track and report on your monthly or quarterly website traffic data? One of the most powerful free tools that can track this for you is Google Analytics (also referred to as "GA").

In the past, setting these systems up in GA was kind of a pain; however, Google recently upgraded its training center, making this process less painful by creating the Analytics Academy. https://goo.gl/SVjdUu

Of course, there are a ton of other web-tracking solutions out there and depending on your business model, some could make more sense for you to set up and use. If you're curious about other solutions, this post from Buffer goes much deeper. https://goo.gl/XFQyU2

However, I still like old faithful, Google Analytics. As a mostly free tool, it's pretty hard to beat with the improvements its recently made to the UI (user interface) and UX (user experience).

With GA, you can set up simple conversion paths to actions (also referred to as goals) that will allow you to track behaviors and help you determine what is happening with website visitors.

Also, if you're running advertising channels (pay-per-click advertising), it's super effective to connect GA to Google AdWords to additionally track ROI on ad spend.

Taking this concept even further, by using CallRail, you can track website conversion paths to organic calls.

Google Search Console

Something all business owners should know about is the often-overlooked add-on or working partner with Google Analytics: Google Search Console.

Google Search Console is a free service offered by Google that helps you monitor and maintain your site's presence in Google search results.

You don't have to sign up for Search Console for your site to be included in Google's search results, but doing so can help you understand how Google views your site and optimize its performance in search results.

This tool can help anyone from generalists to specialists, from newbies to those who are more advanced. Even if you don't think you know anything about Search Console, you should be aware of and familiar with the basics of this tool. Here is a simple overview of what it does. https://goo.gl/JHwA6Z

This way, if you go out and hire someone to do even basic SEO, you will be informed about the basics and be able to see the keyword search results without relying on the vendor you hired.

Remember, the goal here is for you to be in command of your marketing data. At a minimum, you should make sure your site is connected to Search Console or hire a webmaster or marketing specialist to help you set it up. Or, if you're more hands-on, this is a great overview of how to set it up. https://goo.gl/ZYijwu

In addition to knowing this general information, it's a good idea to learn all you can about how your site is performing in search results. This knowledge will help you make better and more informed decisions about your site's performance.

This is the dashboard view of Search Console. Notice you can see total clicks, impressions, average click-through rate, and average position (Fig.9).

Once you've taken the time to get a general overview of your site's rankings, you will begin to greatly value the insights it can provide you.

I use the combined available data that flows from Google Analytics, Search Console, and Google AdWords to build our reports. By combining this data, I can not only track my general KPI numbers for traffic, but I can also further leverage this data by connecting these sources to a third-party tool such as SEMRush, which helps me stay on top of my positions across the various markets.

Not only am I able to monitor ranking positions for my different businesses, I can also build out a competitive analysis matrix to see any current paid ads my competitors may be running and compare dimensions such as their spending levels for PPC advertising or even their ad copy. The SEMRush tool can also deliver updates and reports depending on the setup configuration you choose. See Fig. 10 on pg. 58 for the SEMRush dashboard view.

A SMALL BUSINESS OWNER'S GUIDE TO DIGITAL MARKETING

Search Console Dashboard

FIG. 9 SEARCH CONSOLE

SEMRush Dashboard

Domain Analytics

Domain	Organic Keywords	Organic Traffic
dallasartificialgrasse	47 / 0%	0 / 0%
EstateGreens.com	76 / +22.58%	4 / +300.00%
lasvegasartificialgras	16 / -11.11%	0 / 0%
portlandartificialgra	32 / +45.45%	0 / 0%
smarturf.com	285 / +10.89%	15 / -11.76%
sunburstlandscaping	760 / +12.76%	138 / -22.47%
phoenixartificialgras	26 / +13.04%	0 / 0%
atlantaartificialgras	20 / +42.86%	4 / +33.33%
Heavenlygreens.com	3.0k / +0.60%	2.1k / -36.83%
seattleartificialgrass	2 / 0%	0 / 0%

FIG. 10 SEMRUSH DASHBOARD

There are many different types of tools that SEO agencies can use to monitor your site. Armed with this type of information, you can see the value in knowing how to use them.

6. CRM Integration (Lead & Data Management)

Another key component along the way to taking command of your marketing data is choosing and then using the correct CRM platform for lead management.

There are literally hundreds to choose from, all with different types of bells and whistles. In my opinion, choosing one is directly correlated with your marketing sophistication level and how you drive sales. Many of our clients don't need high-end integrations and function great with the tools I will outline in this chapter. Other companies need a broader-based fully integrated solutions to manage their businesses.

Like I said, it depends.

For example, the case study I outline at https://goo.gl/mXeDuu incorporates the following cloud solution and is exactly how we manage the five-step process outlined in a later section to focus on and manage through the top, middle, and bottom of our business funnel.

> Hubspot (top, middle, marketing automation)

> SalesForce (bottom, sales management, production)

> Invoca (integrated call-tracking to the keyword level)

These solutions work as one system, fully integrated, customized, and mapped to manage each touch point in the top, middle, and bottom of the funnel.

Hubspot, for example, is our content optimization system (COS) platform that tracks every detailed part of our marketing automation into highly customized reporting dashboards.

For Heavenly Greens, the business we're outlining in this book, Hubspot is the backbone of the entire system. Hubspot tracks and manages how all of our content is both distributed and consumed. All of the 27 free guide landing page conversions, associated traffic, blog interactions and social posts, email marketing automation, and website conversion metrics are all monitored by Hubspot.

Once a user opts in, this system begins to engage with his or her prospective buyer's journey with relevant content.

Even more impressive are the inbound tracking capabilities Hubspot has. The system pulls available data points, recent visits, on-page website history, free guide downloads and any available social signals and data points the user may bring along with them into one dashboard. The entire digital footprint our prospect produced visiting our site. #supergeeky.

As you can see, this is a fairly sophisticated level of marketing, and even though Hubspot has a functioning CRM that pulls this data, their CRM would not work for what is required by Heavenly Greens.

Enter Salesforce, an amazing tool we had developed and fully integrated into our systems.

Again, the magic of APIs (discussed in an earlier chapter) enabled these three separate solutions to share data, workflows, and marketing automation.

Since the majority of businesses don't need this level of marketing sophistication out of the gate, I will typically help our clients get started using a combination of cloud services that work together capturing data, managing sales flow, and enabling an effective level of marketing automation.

In fact, most just need to get started and create their first lead-tracking CRM system.

Two of my favorites are Capsule CRM and Base CRM, and the previously mentioned Hubspot offers a free CRM as well.

It's not my first choice as a CRM, but it's hard to argue with free.

It seems like this solution is designed as a freemium play to ultimately be used as an onboarding strategy for the Hubspot marketing platform, which makes complete sense. If you think you're going to need a fully integrated content marketing machine similar to what I outlined in this book, it may be worth checking it out.

Capsule CRM

Capsule CRM also has a free version with limited functionality, while the pro version is only $12. One of the great things about this low-cost solution is its Zapier integrations, which can go a long way solving specific problems on the data management and sales cycle side of things.

Base CRM

This is a more robust solution with a significantly better mobile app. However, Base starts at $45 a month per user.

All three of these solutions work great, and depending on the specific needs of your business, one or the other will typically work for our clients.

Of course, there are hundreds more out there... you just need to explore what would work best for your organization.

Data Management

One note of caution: make sure you choose something that you can grow into, especially if you are introducing these applications into a growing business. Nothing can be more disruptive to an organization than technology changes for your staff.

Also, make sure your existing historic sales and marketing data do not become worthless due to incompatibility issues in the future.

I learned this lesson the hard way by camping out way too long on a CRM database solution that was not engineered for upgrades and exports in the future.

This misstep rendered all of my data frozen in time. We discovered this major issue while looking for new CRM solutions.

I could export the data; the problem was how the data was built to export—rigid and dysfunctional. We tried to properly map the export many times without success. I even hired a custom API developer.

We discovered that the export function was built out but failed to include the "reminder engine" that triggered the next steps in the follow-up process. Even worse, we could not export historical account notes attached to each record.

I can name a big brand you would know that is living this exact nightmare due to legacy database issues because it fell into the same trap. Don't let this happen to you.

Make sure you plan for this. We ended up having to start over completely with Salesforce.

7. Marketing Automation (List Management)

The basic definition of marketing automation refers to software platforms and technologies designed for marketing departments and organizations to more effectively market on multiple channels online (such as email, social media, websites, etc.) and automate repetitive tasks.

This process really starts once you begin developing relevant content that your prospects opt in for.

At this point, the idea is that a system begins to engage the user along the prospective buyer's journey with relevant content, typically by email in an automated fashion.

It's still all about the content your prospects are looking for.

Looking below, you can see that content marketing is the top digital trend for 2017 in this graph by SmartInsights (Fig. 11).

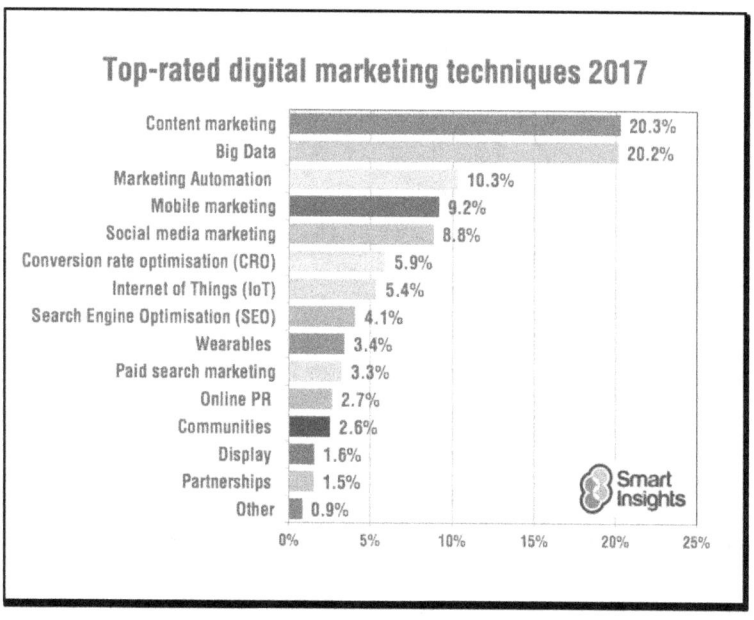

FIG. 11 TREND GRAPH

8. Lead Capture Pages

In order to capitalize on this content marketing trend outlined above in the graph, you need a way to trigger your marketing automation, and that's where your lead capture pages come in.

Once a prospect opts in (provides you with their email address), the next piece of software you need manages your emails. This software triggers automated emails in a timed-based sequence that are designed to nurture your prospects along the buyer's journey with information about your product or service that the buyer has told you they're interested in learning more about.

We call these email systems "Auto Responders," where a pre-defined set of email content can be automatically triggered when someone fills out your form.

This process is called "lead nurturing," and even though everyone today is overwhelmed by email, it's still an effective way to communicate to your prospects, especially if you're giving them the type of content they want.

Obviously, if you're already using one of the bigger marketing automation platforms, this section may not offer anything new; however, if you don't have a lead capture page and related automation in place for your business, this section is for you.

The old school style of lead capture for small business websites was the standard "RFI" (request for information) lead gen form that visitors to your website were expected to fill out. The problem with this approach is that most of the time, your prospects don't want to talk with you... it's too early in "their" buyer's journey, and typically, this is your opportunity to engage them with your with content.

Static web forms are quickly becoming less and less effective. Today's consumers are expecting more and more from websites; they expect answers to the questions they have about your products and services, and that's exactly why content marketing works so well.

For this example, let's assume your business does not have a lead capture page. Here's how this process works.

The easiest way to set up a functional and effective system is to build one by connecting cloud app solutions together.

There are many options available in the market, and depending on what type of business you operate, a solution is out there for you. Here is a a brief list and outline of my go-to tools:

Kajabi

Kajabi is an all-in-one marketing and content delivery platform that is hosted for you, and it is ideal for creating digital products and managing all aspects of digital marketing. With Kajabi, you can seamlessly operate a website and manage all aspects of social media, including blogs, videos, and email.

Kajabi has recently published a number of new jaw-dropping updates to its platform, which has positioned it as a real player among the "all-in-one" type platforms, and with a Zapier integration, this system is one of my favorites.

For example, I use Kajabi to manage the Case Study and Free Marketing Blueprint opt-in landing page at https://goo.gl/mXeDuu. Its also used to manage my other digital businesses.

ClickFunnels

ClickFunnels is another example of an "all-in-one" solution with lots of functionality. One of the biggest reasons I like CF is not only how fast you can deploy these pages, but also the large number of integrations that make this app limitless in terms of functionality.

I use CF in my consulting business as a part of my "done-for-you" bolt-on marketing solutions. With CF, we can create fantastic landing pages and leverage a full suite of integrations from Google Analytics to email auto-responders.

It's a perfect low-cost solution for many of my clients. This is another solution that can manage your business entirely from a marketing perspective.

9. Website Monitoring and Backups

Another often-overlooked item for many small businesses is taking the time to set up a data disaster recovery plan.

Sadly, most owners end up learning this completely avoidable lesson the hard way (myself included). There are so many back up and support solutions out there that I'm not going to go into great detail on this subject.

However, I will admit that it happened to me. Back in 2012, one of my sites was completely hacked and compromised. Of course, we had nothing backed up. Overnight, all of our SERPs (search engine results pages), which amounted to thousands of pages, and all of our organic traffic was being redirected to another country selling knock-off Air Jordans. We were in danger of being de-indexed by Google. Not good.

The only thing saving us was that we had been in production on a new website sitting on the HubSpot servers. Our old site had been mapped and completely indexed a week earlier, which gave me the option of just switching servers. We dodged a major bullet and I learned a major lesson.

The lesson here is to make sure your site is backed up and monitored for hacks. It happens to everyone eventually, so don't get caught without being prepared.

Reach out to your hosting company or marketing partner and get a program in place. Seriously, do it.

10. Set Up Monthly Reporting

It sort of goes without saying that you need to have some sort of monthly reporting of your KPIs in order to properly manage your baseline forecasts.

The first thing you want to get into the habit of doing is setting up some sort of monthly reporting. Depending on which systems you use, the ones on this list or what you have in place, you need to commit to some sort of data-driven report to manage your success metrics.

The 5-Step Outline

Now that we have discussed in great detail how all these systems work together, I would like to describe the five-step process you can put into action in your business.

The glory days of static websites and multi-input lead forms are over as more users demand quick, mobile-friendly, dynamic websites. It's a crazy new world of "information consumption" consumerism.

If you're still using the old school one-dimensional lead-acquisition approach of "just fill out the form," you need to rethink your entire approach because the online marketing world is rapidly changing.

Today's Internet user is a mobile-driven powerhouse with literally millions of options at their fingertips.

Here's a fact: nearly 80% of all consumers research a company or service provider online before making a decision to even engage with them. This gives smart marketers an amazing opportunity to take advantage of marketing information about your product or services.

Stop expecting consumers to drop what they're doing and email or call you because chances are they won't, especially if they are just doing research.

Give them a reason to engage with you, and create the content your specific users want. Start thinking about your website prospects in terms of a sales funnel.

Think of them going through a discovery process, or what we call the "buyer's journey." You can provide content at each level of engagement, broken down into three distinctive parts of your funnel: top, middle, and bottom. When you deploy the power of content marketing (meaning that your prospects engage with the information they want and need), your brand starts to build trust and authority.

When you combine this strategy with marketing automation, you can reap even bigger rewards.

For a free content marketing blueprint that includes graphics and illustrations of this next section visit, https://goo.gl/mXeDuu.

Overview of the 5-Step Content Marketing Blueprint

1. Foundation | Understanding Your Buyer's Journey

The five steps of the website buyer's journey are:

Awareness, engagement, subscription, conversion, and the sale.

However, something to keep in mind is that each of your website visitors are looking for something completely different in their individual journeys. Your website needs to provide information for each of these types of visitors along their way to conversion.

Your goal should be to have your prospects "self-enroll" into your "free information" giveaways and into your marketing automation system.

This is the key to creating a new set of loyal and repeat customers. When your website content provides value in advance, your company can position itself on value as opposed to price.

The more value you can establish in the eyes of the user, the more visitors are compelled to see you as the market authority.

Look at your competition. Are they serving the buyer's journey?

Or are they just expecting users to fill out a form to get their answer? The days of on-page black-and-white marketing are over and gone.

Top | Middle | Bottom

TOFU = Top of the funnel (information gatherers)

Tire kickers, prices shoppers, and non-committed users make up the bulk of everyone's website traffic. Unless you can **make an offer to this group** (such as a free guide, webinar, or video), they leave.

MOFU = Middle of the funnel (free guide downloads)

We take advantage of the "research process" of the buyer's journey and **create segmented audiences,** then nurture them into the next step in your conversion process.

BOFU = Bottom of the funnel (ready to make a buying decision)

This stage is all about creating more qualified buyers by giving your prospects the information they're looking for.

Once they consume your content and end up in your marketing automation, you can become the local market authority to them.

2. Content | Targeting Your Avatar

Creating content is the biggest part of the process.

You need to establish content for the top, middle, and bottom of the funnel, creating content that speaks to each stage.

TOFU = Awareness (information gatherers)

MOFU = Consideration (downloads > email automation)

BOFU = Decision (ready to make a buying decision)

Decide who your target is (specific audience).

Write your web content for this audience.

Create compelling content offers that give value.

Choose the two to five core messages for your avatar.

Select your strategic offering.

For our CTA for the turf business, we used: "Get $500 off Plus a Free Leaf Blower."

Your content should position your product/program/service on value, not price.

3. Evangelize | Publish, Syndicate & Communicate

Repeatedly publishing your content is an essential step. The importance of creating new content (blogs) every month cannot be overstated.

This part of your content marketing strategy pays long-term dividends and also tells Google you're an active publisher of content, which helps to boost your local SEO rank. However, it does not take the place of your SEO program—it's only part of it.

It's critical to make sure your website is attracting interest, getting seen by the search engines, and encouraging the consumption of your free guide content.

Once someone opts into your funnel, you can communicate and build the automated email sequence around it.

Key Items to Keep in Mind:

- Always communicate with your database (list)
- You need to market to your list one time a month at a minimum
- Static websites don't sell, they get forgotten

- Blog to tell your story (no one else is doing it)
- Manage organic traffic with effective SEO
- Paid traffic is a real-time lead-generating opportunity
- Drive paid traffic to your offers through ads & email contacts
- Establish custom digital audiences with retargeting
- Syndicate your blog content
- Maintain and manage your social media
- Never let a comment go without a company response

4. Automate | The Power of a System

Capture pages (sometimes called "landing pages") can:

Grab your website visitor's name and email address, automatically adding them to your email marketing system for automated email follow-ups to your "free guide" downloads.

This is the exact process you can use to systematize your capture pages and automate your free guide delivery.

5. Scale & Optimize | Traffic & Congruency

Paid traffic (driving leads) is by far the quickest way to create leads for your business. Paid traffic is predictable and manageable.

Capture (Grow Your Database)

When you're capturing website visitors into your database by giving away your free content, they don't leave your site empty-handed. Win/Win.

Segment (Separate Your Audience by Interest)

Don't have the same email follow-up message for everyone. Write your content in a structured follow-up sequence.

Convert (Is Your Content Converting?)

Make sure you're taking the time to create compelling email follow-up content that is specific to the guide your prospect has asked for. Otherwise, your open rates and click-through rates will suffer and decline.

In the Trenches

The 5-Step Process in Action

Over the next few sections, I'm going to illustrate for you how the five-step process (using the systems I outlined in this book) are all working together for HeavenlyGreens.com, the very business I outline in greater detail as a case study you can access here: https://goo.gl/mXeDuu.

This is the business that I've talked about throughout this book.

I've used this exact five-step process to drive leads, create more qualified buyers, and average over $10,000,000 in sales each year over the last decade. The process has become more refined, but the framework is exactly as I lay it out for you.

Step 1: The Buyer's Journey

Heavenly Greens is the nation's largest and most successful independent artificial turf installation company. As a GEO fenced business (a local business serving a specific geographic area), our entire customer acquisition process is built around content marketing.

For our prospects, the buyer's journey starts with doing research first, and since we follow the **10-Point Checklist** (which I outlined in an earlier section), our prospects end up on our website doing research on artificial grass.

Typically, these prospects can be segmented into five distinct buyer groups. Over 80% of our business is B to C residential.

A. Home beautification (landscaping)

B. Dog owners

C. Golfers (putting greens)

D. Playgrounds & bocce ball

E. Commercial landscaping

As a result of these five separate avatars, we've created content specifically addressing questions or concerns around these products in the form of 27 different free guides (20 guides shown in Fig. 12).

We also leverage a lot of blog content. In fact, we have a long running joke around here: "What's been a bigger success?" Over $100MM in sales or blogging about artificial grass three times a week for the last decade?

That volume of blogging introduces a lot of content in the market, addressing virtually any research topic that can be searched for.

Plus, each blog is keyword-driven and SEO-optimized with an embedded CTA in each of the posts.

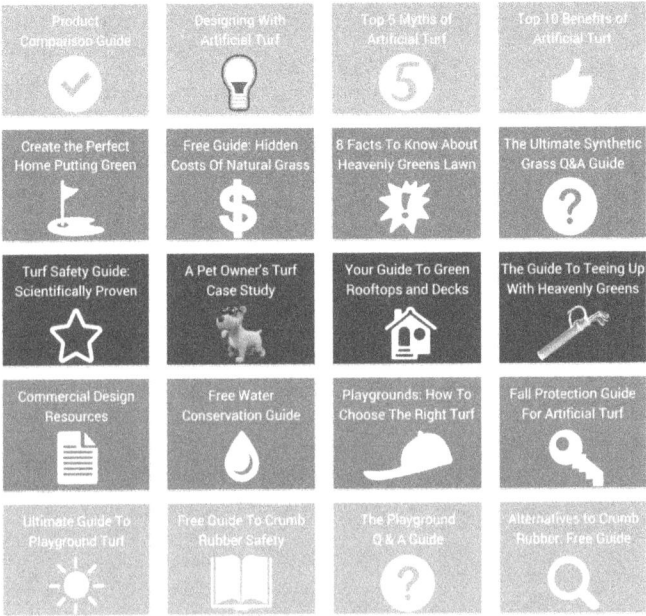

FIG. 12 FREE GUIDES

This content marketing drives free organic leads each and every month (Fig.13).

Step 2: Top, Middle & Bottom of the Funnel

The more content you can give away, the more prospects enter your funnels.

By using this strategy, we're constantly adding prospects to our marketing automation.

In fact, at the time of writing this book, we're seeing a YoY lift in subscribers by +52.62% (Fig. 14).

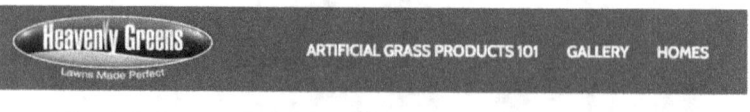

ARTIFICIAL TURF ARTICLES

Fall Sports To Enjoy With Your Friends & Family On Your Artificial Turf

Posted by Troy Scott on 25 August

 Just because the weather is cooling off doesn't mean your family should head indoors and plop down in front of the TV or game console for the next few months. Yes, it's almost time to pack up your favorite summer backyard games. But there's still time to enjoy them as you transition into fall sports. And thanks to your artificial turf, your lawn is sports-ready for family and friends.

   Read More

New Product Alert: Check Out These 5 New Artificial Grasses

Posted by Troy Scott on 24 August

 Artificial grass is a product of science and technology. And since science and technology are constantly evolving, artificial grass is constantly improving. More sophisticated options. More specialized features. Better-than-ever safety and performance characteristics.

  Read More

FIG. 13 BLOGGING

A SMALL BUSINESS OWNER'S GUIDE TO DIGITAL MARKETING 83

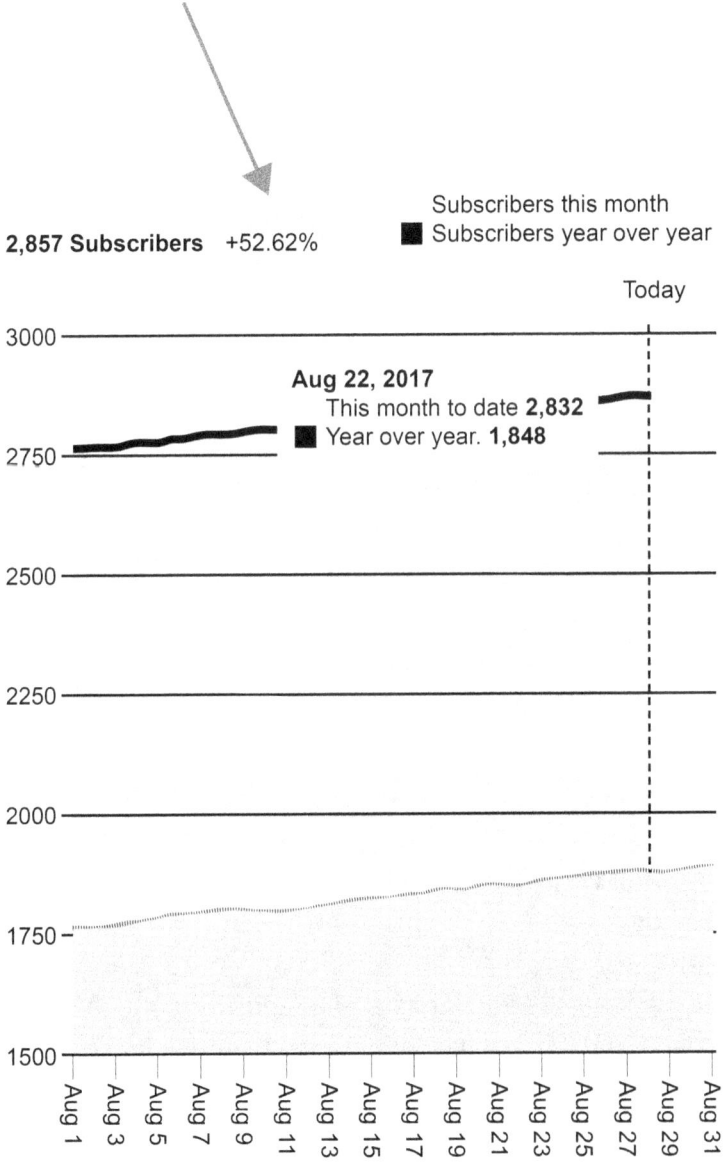

FIG. 14

Step 3: Content Targeting Your Avatar

It makes a lot of sense to build content around your target avatar, not only so you make compelling content but more importantly, so you know who your content is speaking to.

At Heavenly Greens, we focused on one of our core buyers: "Mary." In our market, Mary is the core buyer for the home beautification (landscaping) segment of our five buyer groups.

Here is what we know about Mary:

- Married
- Has two kids and a dog
- Makes over $100k a year
- A director or VP-level employee
- Makes all the buying decisions in the home
- Runs the house
- Does her research
- Is a savvy shopper
- Probably could tell our sales folks about the products in detail
- Is going to get two more bids
- Needs a reason to do business with us

You get the idea. We know this avatar, and we produce our content around her. We use this information to speak in a voice that Mary can hear.

Step 4: Publish, Syndicate & Communicate

You can see from reading above that we produce a lot content. Not only are we sending out content in the form of blogs, we syndicate our content to all the major social media platforms.

Another major part of content syndication is sending thousands of emails with our lead nurturing campaigns (email automation) from free guide downloads.

Looking below, this dashboard shows healthy open and click rates compared to the prior quarter (Fig. 15).

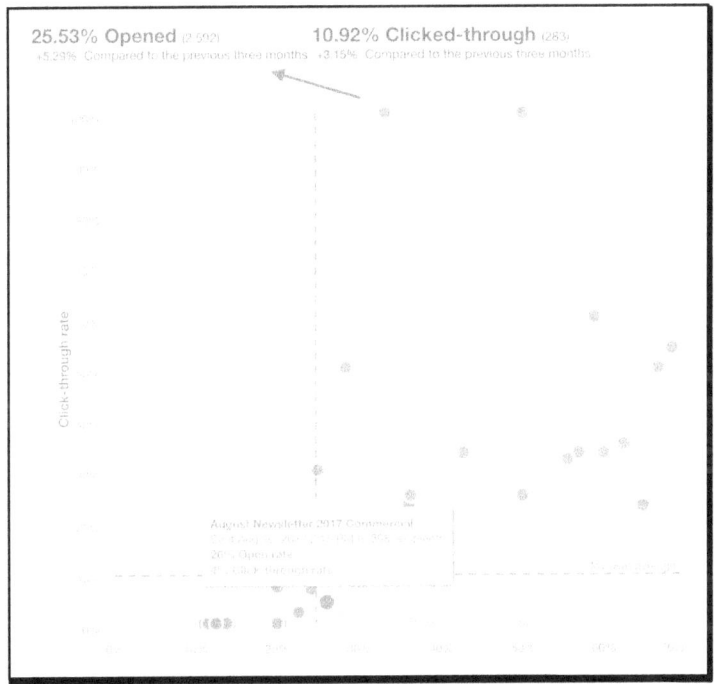

FIG. 15 SUBSCRIPTIONS

Step 5: Scale & Optimize

We spend over $130k a year on Google AdWords, which by some standards is nothing, while for others is a big budget.

We've scaled up our spending considerably over the years. Today, this account is fully optimized down to every keyword, ad group, and successful ad copy data point.

This advertising channel has become a predictable revenue model for us, producing over $1MM in sales like clockwork (Fig.16).

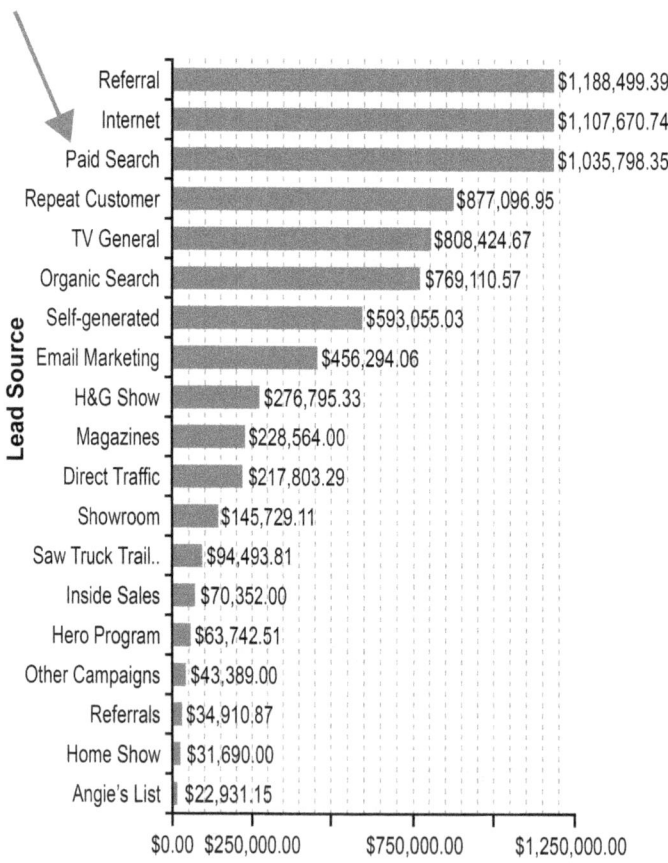

FIG. 16 REVENUE BY SOURCE

Last year's general KPI numbers (Fig.17)

HG' Marketing KPI's for 2016

5,125,032 Digital Ad Impressions

Over 100,000 Website Visits

80,796 Marketing Emails Sent

43,794 PPC Clicks

4,191 Leads Created

Inbound Phone Calls

3,054 Appointments Booked ◄ 76-81% Conv. Rate

2,891 Appointments Ran

830 Sold Contracts

~30+% Closing Rate

FIG. 17 CORE KPIS

Lead Nurturing vs. Buying Leads

Here is a short case study to illustrate the value in giving away free guides to prospects who are opting in for the content you've created and then being nurtured along a buyer's journey versus just buying leads.

This is going to get a little geeky, but it proves the value in content marketing.

This campaign was essentially a contextual ad buy (contextual advertising is advertising on a website that is targeted to be relevant to the page's content) and was completely digital, driving users to a video about artificial grass.

In fact, I was buying traffic that was targeted by user behavior demographics and geo-specific (by city) homeowners who had shown interest in home improvement projects or landscaping.

We built the target audience using homeowner IP addresses within a specific demographic and buying interest compiled as an "output" algorithm made up of collected cookie and browser history. Yup. #supergeeky

In fact, our digital marketing map looked like this:

> > IP Target >> "contextual content targeted" display ad >> **hope for a click** >> pixel the user with remarketing code on landing page >> converted lead >> no conversion >> pixel code snippet shows follow-up display ads for in 30, 45, 60, and 90 days >> follow-up display ad >> campaign ends

The problem is that you have no idea if the prospect is even remotely interested in your product or service. Totally cold traffic.

As a result, you are not in control of the buyer's journey (in fact, we lost control at the "hope for a click step" above), and the campaign turned out to be a complete waste of money.

We didn't even get an opt-in email for future marketing opportunities. A total bust.

This is why content marketing works so well…

Because your content is meeting prospects when they're at the information-gathering stage (top of the funnel), giving away your free guides allows you to create a database of interested prospects.

That in turn, triggers your marketing automation (middle of the funnel) and ultimately creates higher next-step conversion percentages (Heavenly Greens has book to appointment numbers like +75%) and equally consistent opt-in rates.

This shows +30% opt-in rates for those who are ready to make a buying decision (bottom of the funnel) (Fig. 18).

Here is another great case study about lead nurturing for a National brand, Allstate.

https://goo.gl/ZLqtCy

As you can see in those results, content marketing is a fantastic way to nurture lookers into interested buyers.

Top Landing Pages

Date range: This year so far

NAME	TOTAL VIEWS	TOTAL CONVERSION RATE
1. Free Guide: Heaven...	8,099	6%
2. Special Offer $500 ...	5,250	1%
3. 8 Facts You Should ...	2,682	3%
4. The Ultimate Synthe...	1,801	5%
5. Request a Quote for...	1,773	33%

FIG. 18 OPTIN RATES

With all of this information, you have a few things to consider before you map out and build your digital marketing plan.

Here are few questions to ask yourself before you get started.

10-Step Quick Start Guide

Step One: Begin by knowing what you want to achieve and understanding why your customers come to you.

Step Two: Know how much you can afford to spend per week, month, quarter, or year on digital marketing.

Step Three: Based on that budget, decide whether you'll be doing your own marketing, paying a marketing service, or hiring a marketing employee.

Step Four: Get a mobile-friendly company website online—one that works well on smartphones and desktop computers.

Step Five: Add content, capture pages, and marketing automation using blogs, free guides, and videos for offers.

Step Six: Make sure your business info is active and listed correctly on online business listing sites like Google My Business, Manta, YP.com, and others (there are more than 50 out there).

Step Seven: Set up a Facebook page for your business, then add your company to other social media sites your customers are likely to use. Then start to syndicate your content.

Step Eight: Pay attention to your website traffic using Google Analytics.

Step Nine: Pay attention to your social media activity using the analytic tools built into sites like Facebook, Twitter, Instagram, and LinkedIn.

Step Ten: Depending on how well these tactics are working to bring more sales in your door, decide whether to add paid advertising to your digital marketing plan.

The Power of Outsourcing Your Marketing

As you can imagine, setting up and running these types of systems can not only overwhelm you and your business, the tasks associated with the implementation, creation, and management of content plus tracking and reporting can become an instant roadblock, which typically results in nothing getting done.

Business owners have many things in common and there is quite possibly one universal truth: at some point, each of us will get hit in the face with the universal one-two punch.

The first punch comes when your personal bandwidth hits a ceiling. When you finally realize you really **can't do it all by yourself**.

The second punch is discovering you actually have a time management problem.

Today, this challenge can be overcome by leveraging virtual assistants and growing your team in a way that can actually scale your business much faster than you could all by yourself.

However, most of us will need to get punched first.

For some reason, many entrepreneurs have this intense desire to do everything themselves.

I don't know where that comes from. Maybe it's out of fear that the task will not be done right if we don't do it. Still, for others (yup, I went through this too), it becomes a grappling match with the art of perfectionism.

This one is a killer. It can keep businesses from growing or running more efficiently and can limit any action being taken to bring an idea to light, or worse… it just paralyzes you.

I've been through all of that too, and if any of these issues are holding you back, my advice is to just get it published, launched, or whatever action best fits your situation.

Having a product in the market beats perfection by a long shot because generating revenue wins 100% of the time. Getting your product or service to market is way more important than holding onto the "it's not perfect yet" fallacy.

Here's the truth: it will never be perfect… why do you think they have a version 2.0 for everything?

By outsourcing your marketing, your business can leverage additional marketing support and, in turn, make you more money as a result.

As far back as 2009, I started experimenting with the concept of outsourcing my marketing efforts.

As I mentioned at the beginning of this book, I was doing everything and getting burnt out. I simply could not keep up with running the department and doing everything else on my own.

Over the next few years, I began to look for other ways to get my content created, to have someone else manage my Google AdWords and take over running all the live promotional events throughout the year. Finding the right people or the right companies to manage things wasn't a lot of fun, and sadly, many did not work out.

Finally, after hiring and firing a handful of agencies to manage various responsibilities over the next few years, I wouldn't really find my sweet spot until 2014.

I can unequivocally say without a single doubt that 2014 was the year I fully embraced the concept of outsourcing marketing.

When I combined my expertise with other people's expertise and just let go, not only did I get my time back, in this example, I grew revenues by $2.1 million in only 11 months. The result was spectacular.

However, it's important to note that this result was a by-product of me being quite obsessive at first. I was doing all the work by myself, trusting no one, and taking the time to set it up right.

In fact, I spent more than two years getting it figured out before I let go of anything. Today, I have leverage and scale because I outsourced my marketing.

The $2.1MM Case Study (Enter "The Buyer's Journey")

Back in 2014, one of the best business decisions I made was letting go of the day-to-day content-creating marketing duties for Heavenly Greens and focused squarely on the core KPIs of the business.

As you will see in the article below, I set up the all the systems and marketing automation years prior and was already successful to a certain extent.

The moral of the story here is that when I got out of my own way, let go of the details, and trusted another expert... I got more things done with better results.

I'm lucky because I get to work with a lot of cool companies, and OverGo Studio is no different. Back in 2014, when I was already having great results using inbound content marketing strategies (the five-step process I outline in this book), the problem was creating content, managing workflow, and balancing my other businesses.

I used the power of outsourcing marketing for the best of both worlds. Here is a case study showing you how I gained $2.1 million in additional revenue in one year by leveraging marketing automation.

https://goo.gl/eis18J

The $2,495 Per Month Employee

The ideal candidate, the ever-elusive marketing assistant, is quite hard to find.

I always leaned on the idea that I could just hire my way out of bandwidth issues. At least that's what I assumed. Turns out, that was a bad assumption. In fact, it was just part of poor planning on my end.

The truth is that unless you know exactly what you need to hire for, you'll be forced to go through a number of candidates before you can actually get what you need in terms of production.

When it comes to finding and hiring the right marketing person (one who is well educated about the requirements of today's digital marketing trends), it can get pretty tough.

I've tried it many times, starting with interns right out of college.

Most did not have the skills I needed to hit the ground running right out of the gate, which I understand, but I needed a turn-key solution to these problems.

After many attempts, I've only been successful once. In fact, this person continues to be an integral part of my businesses and has become a great friend.

However, today's educated digital marketers are in high demand.

In fact, take a look at this link from DigitalMarketer. It's a great blog post that outlines the costs of hiring competent folks to manage the following important aspects of your digital marketing needs. Check out the infographic: https://goo.gl/ZSUaht

- Content marketing
- Social media marketing
- Video marketing

- Media buying/traffic acquisition
- Testing & optimization
- Email marketing

The costs range from $30,000 a year to $115,000 a year.

After going through the painful process of looking for vendors and working with a variety of different types of agencies, I was surprised that I could not find a true top-to-bottom support service package for small businesses.

Sure, you can find lots of different companies that can support a large swath of needs, but generally speaking, most small business owners are left to fend for themselves when it comes to setting up the type of marketing systems that they need.

More specifically, I wanted to see a support services package that checked off each of the items that I listed on the top ten checklist outlined earlier in the book:

1. Content creation (blogging/free guides/newsletters)
2. Search Engine Optimization (60-point build-out)
3. PPC AdWords management (landing pages)
4. Dynamic call tracking & recording
5. Web traffic & conversion metrics
6. CRM integration (lead management)
7. Marketing automation with email follow-up to segment
8. Lead capture pages for free guides
9. Website monitoring and backup systems
10. Monthly reporting

These are the components that every small business owner needs to have in place in order to achieve baseline and drive a successful digital marketing plan.

Since I could not find a specific solution in the marketplace to address these 10 key elements, I went out and built a "suite of services" package that solved this problem by addressing these needs head-on.

I launched the first version of this service in 2015 (remember, there is always a version 2.0), and over the years, I have slowly perfected the program to where it is today with the capabilities of offering 37 different types of marketing services for small businesses.

Beyond that, we've created a service called the *$2,495 Per Month Employee*. We call it the **Benchmark Marketing Package**.

Essentially, the service is a done-for-you, all-in-one marketing solution that gives small businesses all of the digital tools I talk about in this book as a turn-key monthly support program.

At $2,495 per month, this service is designed as a bolt-on solution that works with just about any website or business as an automated managed marketing system.

I'd love to tell you all about it and give you direct access to my Content Marketing Blueprint and free case studies.

Just visit https://goo.gl/mXeDuu to learn more.

Real Case Studies of Success (Free Videos)

Simply visit https://goo.gl/mXeDuu to access these free case studies, and download your free Content Marketing Blueprint. Don't forget to check out the *$2,495 Per Month Employee!*

1) **A $100,000,000 Marketing Machine**
   Video Case Study of HeavenlyGreens.com

2) **From Zero to 7 Figures with Paid Traffic**
   Video Case Study of a Local Retail Business

3) **Increasing Local Organic Traffic with SEO**
   Video Case Study of Growing Organic Lead-flow

I sincerely hope the information contained in the book will help you grow your business, improve the visibility of your business online, and provide you with the tools you can use to take command of your marketing data.

Thank you for taking the time to read this book.

All the best,

Troy S. Scott

About the Author

Troy Scott is a Best Selling Author, Speaker, Entrepreneur and Digital Marketing Expert.

As a former startup junky living in Silicon Valley he grew tired of the boom-bust cycle of chasing the ultimate "MVP" (minimal viable product) and the mad rush required to market it. He transitioned his diverse marketing skills into helping other entrepreneurs set up proven online systems that grow their businesses faster and easier.

www.ingramcontent.com/pod-product-compliance
Lightning Source LLC
Chambersburg PA
CBHW050112230526
45470CB00004B/1802